The Faith of Jesus

Saying Yes to God's Love

by
Herbert E. Douglass

TEACH Services, Inc.
PUBLISHING
www.TEACHServices.com ◆ (800) 367-1844

Copyright © 2015 Herbert E. Douglass
and TEACH Services, Inc.

ISBN-13: 978-1-4796-0501-9
Library of Congress Control Number: 2001091811

Published by

TEACH Services, Inc.
PUBLISHING
www.TEACHServices.com • (800) 367-1844

Table of Contents

Chapter One

THE URGENT IMPORTANCE OF FAITH

REMEMBER that night on the Sea of Galilee after a bone-wearying day when the storm swept down from the hills, tossing our Lord's boat like a cork, swamping it with water? The disciples were desperate, while the Lord slept. Their best efforts seemed useless. When all seemed lost, they remembered on whose mission they were. They turned to Him in their great need. "Master, Master, we are perishing!" (Luke 8:24, RSV*).

Awakened by the cry of panic, Jesus stood in that tossing boat, raised His hand to the angry sea, and asked for peace. The clouds broke, the sea calmed, and the disciples, together with traveling companions in nearby boats, watched in astonishment. No doubt they smothered Jesus with gratitude and praise.

But was amazement and praise what Jesus wanted from His fellow travelers in that hour of peril and deliverance? "Where is your faith?" He asked. His emphasis was on *your.*

Jesus, as the Man among men, was making a vitally important point. He had rested in the stern of that boat, wrapped in peace, without a trace of fear in His heart. But His peace was not because He faced the peril as God. He met the storms and pressures of life with the same human liabilities shared by the others in the boat. As a man, He slept, though He encountered the terrors common to humanity. But as a man, Jesus slept *in faith* in the sustaining power of His heavenly Father. The power that stilled the storm was not His own but was that of His Father in heaven.

How He reacted to peril was the way all men and women may face difficulties—that way, His way, is the natural outworking of

*All Bible quotations not otherwise specified are from the Revised Standard Version.

1

the life of faith. "As Jesus rested by faith in the Father's care, so we are to rest in the care of our Saviour. If the disciples had trusted in Him, they would have been kept in peace.... Living faith in the Redeemer will smooth the sea of life, and will deliver us from danger in the way that He knows to be best" *(The Desire of Ages,* p. 336).*

What Jesus desired in His disciples on that black night was faith—a trust and a habit pattern that would reflect the way He met life's problems. In His question appears a mild reproof, "Where is *your* faith?"

He still rebukes men and women when they fear that they cannot be like Him. Any self-serving, comfortable thought that we can not "be like him" (1 John 3:2) this side of the resurrection will again receive His condemnation. Such strange defeatism places a low estimate on His grace, a low expectation on what He can do for His friends. If His grace and example are to mean anything, He does not expect His followers to spend the rest of their lives in some kind of pious apology for failing to do what He says man can do by the same divine-human cooperation He experienced.[1]

Astonishment, even praise, is not what Jesus wants. It does not please Jesus as it would a magician, who performs many surprising things to dazzle and awe men and women. Luke reported that the disciples "were afraid, and they marveled" (Luke 8:25). Fearful disciples, apologetic piety, and even grateful appreciation for what He has done do not best reflect our Lord's glory or His power as the Saviour of men and women.

---

*All quotations not otherwise specified are from the writings of E. G. White.

[1]"Let no one say, I cannot remedy my defects of character. If you come to this decision, you will certainly fail of obtaining everlasting life. The impossibility lies in your own will. If you will not, then you can not overcome. The real difficulty arises from the corruption of an unsanctified heart, and an unwillingness to submit to the control of God....

"As the will of man cooperates with the will of God, it becomes omnipotent. Whatever is to be done at His command may be accomplished in His strength. All His biddings are enablings" *(Christ's Object Lessons,* pp. 331-333).

"Through the Spirit the believer becomes a partaker of the divine nature. Christ has given His Spirit as a divine power to overcome all hereditary and cultivated tendencies to evil, and to impress His own character upon His church" *(The Desire of Ages,* p. 671).

People who do not know the Lord do well to be afraid in the face of illness and natural calamities. It is no surprise if uncommitted men and women cringe like slaves before the anguish of personal disasters or in the clutch of self-destroying evil habits. But should Christians? Not if they have the faith of Jesus!

If one text identifies God's people in the last days, distinguishing them from the world and nominal church members, it would probably be Revelation 14:12: "Here is a call for the endurance of the saints, those who keep the commandments of God and the faith of Jesus." The passage describes those who have responded to the "judgment hour" messages of the three angels (Revelation 14:1-11), messages that the world has heard since 1844. It identifies those people prepared for Jesus to come, ready to be translated.

Such people are the harvest of the gospel seed for which Jesus now waits. Their public witness becomes God's last plea to a rebel planet. When everyone living at the same time around the world finally accepts or rejects the call God makes through their word and example, He can say or do nothing more to make His invitation any clearer. Probation then closes. That is why the next event described in Revelation 14 is the return of Jesus.

The question is: How do we join this group—that is, the people who keep the commandments of God and the *faith of Jesus?*

Apparently such people do not become God's Exhibit A without *endurance.* They bear difficulties creatively, with dignity, even with joy. Cheerfully they tell the world by their words and lives that whatever happens, Jesus is more than able to keep them from falling, that His strength is sufficient for all things.

God's people are also *commandment-keepers.* No ifs, ands, and buts—the Bible says that they are commandment-keepers. Although glad to forgive, God is even more pleased to give power to cleanse His people from their sins, to assist them in being overcomers and commandment-keepers, because that is what being a Saviour is all about (Matthew 1:21). No question about it, God's people will be commandment-keepers, trophies of His grace and power forever (Ephesians 1:6, 12; 2:10, 14-21).

But such people do not *endure* crushing burdens and the "flaming darts of the evil one," they do not truly *keep the commandments,* unless they have the *faith of Jesus.* Only this faith will develop durable, lovable, winsome commandment-keepers.

The faith of Jesus is saving faith.[2] Such faith saved Jesus from sin. It protected Him from feeling sorry for Himself, kept Him unspotted from the world.[3] By faith He "grew in wisdom and stature, and in favor with God and men" (Luke 2:52, NIV*)—a powerful, gracious person. This kind of faith will do the same for you and me.[4] The faith of Jesus produces the character of Jesus—and it is the character of Jesus that all heaven waits to see reproduced in those people who call themselves commandment-keepers and heralds of the Advent.[5]

A towering urgency has rested upon each generation since 1844 to understand and experience "the faith of Jesus." Not only the completion of God's last call to a needy world but also the well-being of every professed Christian here and now depends upon it. So does each person's eternal destiny. We need to discover for ourselves what it means to live by faith as Jesus did. We need, more than all else, the "faith of Jesus."

---

[2]"As the Son of God lived by faith in the Father, so are we to live by faith in Christ. So fully was Jesus surrendered to the will of God that the Father alone appeared in His life. Although tempted in all points like as we are, He stood before the world untainted by the evil that surrounded Him. Thus we also are to overcome as Christ overcame" *(ibid., p. 389).*

[3]"By faith He rested in Him whom it had ever been His joy to obey. And as in submission He committed Himself to God, the sense of the loss of His Father's favor was withdrawn. By faith, Christ was victor" *(ibid., p. 756).*

*From the New International Version. Copyright © 1973 by The New York Bible Society International and is used by permission.

[4]"Christ did not fail, neither was He discouraged, and His followers are to manifest a faith of the same enduring nature. They are to live as He lived, and work as He worked, because they depend on Him as the great Master Worker... They are to have power to resist evil, . . . power that will enable them to overcome as Christ overcame" *(ibid., pp. 679, 680).*

[5]"Christ is waiting with longing desire for the manifestation of Himself in His church. When the character of Christ shall be perfectly reproduced in His people, then He will come to claim them as His own" *(Christ's Object Lessons, p. 69).*

God is not asking us to emulate the faith of Abraham, even though Scripture calls him the "Father of the faithful." He is not even holding up Moses as the high challenge before the last generation, although many of us would settle for his endurance and fidelity. Though they put our faith to shame, neither Abraham nor Moses had the faith that will characterize "those who keep the commandments of God and the faith of *Jesus*."

It will take the faith of Jesus to withstand the evil one during the pressures and final assaults of the last days. Cut off from every means of earthly support, surrounded by loved ones and friends who plead for moderation and compromise, God's people will endure and face misunderstanding and terror triumphantly—because they, too, have developed in their own experience the same kind of faith that preserved Jesus from flinching under similar attacks from friends and foes alike.

"Where is *your* faith?" Here is the question that Jesus asks those who long for the Advent. Out of that large group the world over who talk and sing about being ready for the Advent, there will come a smaller group who will understand our Lord's question. Their answer is a life of faith—an overcoming, triumphant life that reflects their Lord's example. John portrays them with those galvanizing words: "Here they are—those who keep the commandments of God and the faith of Jesus" (Revelation 14:12).

Chapter Two

HOW FAITH IS MISUNDERSTOOD

S O far we have been describing the importance of faith—especially for those who want to comprise part of God's people ready for His second advent. But, if such faith is so important, why don't we see more of it? Because Christians generally are stiff-necked and evil? Hardly. Part of the problem stems from the fact that some people think they have faith when they don't. Others assume they don't need faith because they believe there is a more mature way to render glory to God. Then again, many misunderstand the nature of salvation because they have a wrong conception of what faith is. All this within Christianity, all claiming Jesus as their Saviour.

For example, many people feel that the church has flailed the doctrine of righteousness by faith to pieces. They argue, "We have heard the subject for years." Bored, they consider the subject elementary. But such boredom represents evidence enough that they have missed the crucial subject's meaning.

One of the chief causes of such boredom on one hand, or the recurring controversies on the other, whenever church members discuss the doctrine of righteousness by faith is that the focus usually centers on terms such as "Justification," "sanctification," or even "righteousness"—*all the while assuming that they well understand the nature of faith.* Most discussions about such terms generally flounder into impersonal Bible studies or simple frustration, not primarily because of the man-made difficulties that have become associated with theological terms such as "justification by faith," "sanctification by faith," "righteousness by faith," but because of an unconscious assumption that everyone knows what faith means in the formulas. An inadequate conception has distorted the terms, subjecting them to enormous theological wrangling.

Basic to our problem is that most any Christian believes he has faith. But in that belief lies the cause of the conflict and confusion of the centuries. Many definitions of faith exist. Often they contradict each other. The fundamental misunderstanding of faith is one of the crucial reasons, not only for the multiplicity of Christian churches, but also for the wide variances in interpreting almost every Biblical doctrine.

Think how the misunderstanding of faith has helped to divide Christians on such subjects as these:

- Sovereignty of God and the responsibility of man
- The nature of Jesus' humanity
- Predestination and freedom
- Atonement—subjective, objective, or both
- Image of God—what was lost, and what can be restored in this life
- Nature of sin—substantive or relational
- Church—fellowship or institution, organism or organization
- Bible—inerrant transcription, a divine human instrument of communication and faith, or a human record of a religious people
- Sacraments—mystical magic or symbols of worship
- Church offices—hierarchical authority or service functions
- Preaching—transmission of information or personal encounter

Think of the many ways we casually use the word *faith:*

1. "We don't have enough information—we must go ahead on faith." But faith is not a blind leap we try when all else fails.

2. "He is a Baptist; he doesn't belong to the Methodist faith." Faith is more than a body of religious information.

3. "Keep the faith, baby!" Heard most frequently during the 1960s and early 1970s, the slogan suggests that one equates faith with deep loyalties. However, Christian faith is more than intense conviction. If not, then devoted followers of Chairman Mao or Adolf Hitler represent shining examples for Christians to emulate.

4. "I have faith that technology will find a solution to the energy crisis before the world runs out of oil and gas." Yet faith is more than confidence in the scientific process, more than trust in the painstaking effort and methods associated with the remarkable successes of the laboratory.

5. "We should be traveling northwest, but if we have faith in our compass, we should make a turn now because it says that we are really going east." At least such faith rests in something objective, outside of whims or deep conviction, even though our faith in the compass calls us to act contrary to our own experience. Does faith exist if we do not change our direction of travel?

6. "This car surely looks well cared for, but I don't know anything about buying cars. I will take it to Leonard—I have faith in his judgment when it comes to automobiles." Here faith involves trusting someone else's judgment, and his decision may be sufficient for buying cars. But is such second-hand faith sufficient when we consider marriage, joining a church, a family life-style, or which day is the Sabbath in the twentieth century?

7. "I never thought that I would get a brain tumor. However, my neurosurgeon will pull me through the operation—I have faith in him." More than a compass, more than a friend's judgment about buying a car, we now place our life into the skilled hands of a trained surgeon. Unfortunately he is another human being with all the high and low days that afflict any other individual.

At random we have looked at a number of ways whereby we use the word *faith.* Although some of the instances seem to share certain aspects in common, each occasion is singularly different. But we are still employing the same word *faith.* Try to substitute in the phrase "righteousness by faith" the definition of faith contained in any one of the seven examples. Now we begin to see the problem that unconsciously burdens us as we seek for that quality that will distinctively mark God's people in the last days. Consequently, we must understand what the Bible means when it uses *faith,* for none of our customary definitions could possibly help us.*

Part of our present confusion results from our contemporary languages (English, French, German) as we try to translate the Greek words *pistis* (noun) and *pisteuein* (verb). The noun *pistis* (generally by "faith" in English) is most often translated into Latin as *fides;* into French as *foi*, into German as *Glaube.*

But these languages (with the exception of German) have done something to an understanding of "faith" that the Greek knew better *not* to do—they separated the noun from the verb. The Greek knew immediately that the "act of faith" (the verb action) was something that the man or woman of "faith" (subject) *did!* Their language was clear: *pistis* was "faith" and *pisteuein* was what faith did. Something similar occurs in English—the writer writes; the swimmer swims; the fearful fear.

But in translating *pistis* and *pisteuein,* most modern languages separated the noun from the verb so that the connection between the two becomes unrecognizable in the translation. Even worse is that the gulf between the noun and verb did not arise by accident. Languages do not make up words without reason. Because people eventually misunderstood the *meaning* of Christian "faith," because theology became confused as to what faith meant, the language reflected it. For example: the Latin for *pistis* is *fides,* but its verb counterpart is *credere,* creating a serious gap for misunderstanding as we shall see in a moment. The French for *pistis* is *foi,* but its verb is *croire;* the English translates *pistis* with

---

*When we turn to the English Bible, for example, to discover what *faith* means, we do not suggest that a word necessarily has only one meaning or that the sense of any passage depends upon the invariable definition of a key word. Especially is this true when we are using translations and not the Greek of the New Testament and the Hebrew of the Old. We are emphasizing, however, that a word derives its meaning primarily from its context, that a comparison of several usages of that word in each context will help clarify with greater precision the general definition of a particular word. In addition, a later inspired writer will clarify a Biblical word in certain contexts, providing us with an even less subjective basis for interpretation.

"faith" and its verb counterpart (especially in the King James Version) is "to believe."

The unfortunate cleavage between noun and verb has led the unsuspecting through the centuries into a profound miscomprehension of the New Testament concept of faith. For example, the Latin *credere* means "to give credit to, to assent to, a doctrine or belief" Thus a person can believe a statement without having any particular personal relationship to it, without any special change of life-style because of a mental acceptance. When one uses *credere* (Latin) or *croire* (French) or "to believe" to translate the Greek verb *pisteuein* (to have faith) something perverse and alien to the simple but important concept of New Testament faith has occurred.

In John 3:16, "For God so loved the world that he gave his only Son, that whoever believes in him should not perish but have eternal life," the average person would associate "believe" with intellectual acknowledgment, as we would when asked to believe that Jesus was resurrected on Sunday morning and not Tuesday morning. Barring a few exceptions, in every instance where the King James Version (and many other English translations or versions as well) uses "believe," it is translating *pisteuein,* the Greek verb, "to have faith."

The German language has done something even more interesting with the concept of faith. Although it has not separated the noun from the verb *(Glaube—glauben),* the linguistic tragedy still exists. Teaching the weekly Bible lesson to a group of elderly Germans in North Dakota brought it forcibly to my mind. We were discussing faith. I asked them to tell me in German, "I have faith in Jesus." Dutifully they said, "Ich glaube an Jesus." Then I requested them to say, "I believe you have blue eyes." They started, "Ich glaube . . ." Pausing, they glanced at each other, tried several ways, and finally one commented, "Either we have no word for *believe* or we have no word for *faith*." And they took several moments to buzz among themselves at the plight they were in.

The problem has been that over the years the German word *Glaube* strongly tends to be associated only with an intellectual process, thus equating faith with mental belief, that man's primary response to God is "to believe." But such an unconscious equating of faith with intellectual belief is also part of the English and French mind as well.

When Paul and Silas told the jailer, "Believe on the Lord Jesus Christ, and thou shalt be saved" (Acts 16:31, KJV), the apostles did not mean that merely assenting to the fact that Jesus was God, that He was crucified, that He promised to forgive our sins, is man's only part in his salvation. A more accurate translation would read, "Have faith in the Lord Jesus Christ." As we shall see, such faith consists of much more than agreement with a set of facts, more than mental conviction, more than a passive acceptance of God's work for us without an active cooperation on our part as we meet the conditions for God's gifts.

The major reason for the general misunderstanding of "faith" (and thus that which lies behind the linguistic confusion) is that a radical misunderstanding has arisen about how God goes about saving men and women—a misconception that existed long before Jesus lived and died. The unfortunate perversion early permeated the Christian church. Even though the church retained the Biblical words, they remained as misplaced labels, pasted on the emerging new perversions of doctrine. Such terms as "faith," "love," and "church" received new meanings because basic Christian principles had become polluted.

So the question becomes even more important in view of the historical misunderstanding. What does *faith* mean? If God asks for more than mental assent or conviction, *what is it? How* does a correct conception of faith affect our view of justification by faith, righteousness by faith, or "the faith of Jesus" in Revelation 14:12? In what way has the distortion of faith led to the distortion of almost every other Biblical doctrine?

Chapter Three

WHAT, THEN, IS BIBLICAL FAITH?

A S we have seen, we daily use the word *faith* to describe many human emotions, ranging from casual belief to deep conviction. We also noted that we employ faith to depict a person's relationship to good people as well as to bad. In other words, we habitually handle *faith* in a general way without precision of meaning, even as we have misused the word love.[1]

In general, faith describes a mental process by which we believe something on the basis of evidence or authority on which we have placed value and act accordingly. That evidence or authority may, or may not, be in itself trustworthy, that is, "truly worth our faith." Mankind has done many foolish and even horrible deeds, as well as a long list of commendable acts, in the name of sincere faith. But faith as a mental process is not good or bad, right or wrong. It is simply that process by which a person believes what seems to him or her to be believable, and acts accordingly. The value of a person's faith depends upon what he or she chooses to believe. Its worth depends upon the quality of person or concept that commands or evokes conviction, allegiance, and commitment.

Consequently, error does not become truth merely because a person has faith in it. Faith in error will not produce the fruit of truth no matter how sincere a person may be. One author said it well: "Faith is the medium through which truth or error finds a lodging place in the mind. It is by the same act of mind that truth or error is received, but it makes a decided difference whether we

---

[1]Something unfortunate has happened to the meaning of "love" when we say, I *love* strawberry shortcake," "I *love my son*," "*I love my* wife," I *love* western sunsets," "I *love* to be left alone," "Make *love, not* war."

believe the Word of God or the sayings of men" *(Selected Messages,* Book One, p. 346).

Biblical faith, however, is specific and unique. It describes the person who chooses to believe, trust, and obey God. This principle is vital—the object of faith determines its value. Thus, it is very important that what we believe, what we have faith in, is really the truth!

Perhaps the only categorical Biblical definition of faith appears in Hebrews 11, verse 1: "Faith is being sure of what we hope for and certain of what we do not see" (NIV).

Then the author, knowing that a cold definition would never suffice, hastens to write a long chapter that has become a classic in world literature. He pictures it in three dimensions, in living color.

"By faith" we learn that "men of old received divine approval" (verse 2); "Abel offered to God a more acceptable sacrifice" (verse 4); "Enoch was taken up so that he should not see death" (verse 5); "Noah ... constructed an ark; ... by this he condemned the world and became an heir of the righteousness which comes by faith" (verse 7); "Abraham obeyed; ... and he went out, not knowing where he was to go" (verse 8); "Sarah herself received power to conceive" (verse 11); "Moses, when he was born, was hid for three months by his parents" (verse 23); "Moses, when he was grown up, refused to be called the son of Pharaoh's daughter" (verse 24); "he left Egypt, not being afraid of the anger of the king" (verse 27); "the people crossed the Red Sea" (verse 29); "the walls of Jericho fell down" (verse 30); men and women "conquered kingdoms, enforced justice, received promises, stopped the mouths of lions, quenched raging fire, escaped the edge of the sword, won strength out of weakness, became mighty in war, put foreign armies to flight" (verses 33, 34).

Such men and women were uncommon heroes of their generation. They did not fade into the wallpaper or blend into the spirit of their age. Although it is easy to remember them for their remarkable achievements, we must never forget that it was their faith that made them what we honor them for. When we review the results of faith that God approves, it is obvious that faith consists of something more than mere mental belief, even more than enthusiasm and zeal. Faith for the Biblical stalwarts was the way—*the only right way*—for each of them to relate to God. It involved (a) a correct understanding of God's plan for them, (b) the will to respond as He wanted, and (c) an abiding trust that He would continue to do His part if human beings would do theirs.

For all the Biblical heroes, faith was saying "yes" to God, to whatever He commanded. Faith was belief, trust, obedience, and deepest conviction all wrapped up in a cheerful companionship with their Lord and Master.

In analyzing Paul's definition of faith in Hebrews 11:1, and his subsequent description throughout the chapter, it helps to note that the word *hupostasis* in verse 1 translated "substance" (KJV), or "assurance" (RSV), or "being sure of" (NIV) means literally, "something placed under," that is, a foundation, or basis. New Testament times often employed the same Greek word as the name for the title deed by which a person proved his ownership of property. The piece of paper, the title deed, was not the property owned, but it represented that property. The owner's basis for confidence, it served as valid proof that the property existed and that the possessor owned it, whether he had ever seen the property or not.

The word *elegchos* also in verse 1, translated "evidence" (KJV), or "conviction" (RSV), or "being certain of" (NIV), refers to anything that serves to convince or persuade.

Thus, in the Bible, the definition of faith includes a "heart" certainty as well as mental conviction. Biblical faith "knows." On the basis of what the Scriptures say about God, He is worth trusting. Everything learned through the faith experience is deeply and firmly persuasive.

By faith, whatever God has promised, we already possess in part because we have already experienced it in part (Ephesians 1:13, 14, 17-19; 2 Corinthians 1:22; 1 John 2:3–6). Thus we can enjoy future promises to some degree now. That kind of assurance was deeply satisfying to an otherwise sad Adam, to an otherwise baffled Abraham, to an Isaiah or Jeremiah who otherwise saw only futility and defeat.

Whatever the subtle arguments of earthly logic, whatever the stony silence that human eyes and ears perceive in the search for meaning by laboratory investigation alone, the man or woman of faith has good reasons for the conclusions of their faith.

As we perceive in the descriptions of men and women of faith in Hebrews, Biblical faith involves the intellect, the will, and the commitment. But it is none of them in themselves. Such faith is simply the whole man saying yes to God, knowing by objective evidence and personal experience that there is nothing deceptive, unreal, or empty about what God has said or what he has experienced. The man or woman of faith knows that God is worth believing, worth trusting, worth obeying, because he or she has learned assurance by personally believing, trusting, and obeying.[2]

Throughout the Bible, *faith* is the English word used to describe a person's proper response to his Creator and Redeemer: "And without faith it is impossible to please him" (Hebrews 11:6). Those of faith please God because they have learned to trust Him as a caring Father. They open their lives so that He can freely share His riches with them, providing for their special needs in a wicked world. Faith calls for a person's intellect, will, and trust.

In fact, men and women of faith simply live to please their Heavenly Father. Pleasing God is their highest, most compelling motivation.

---

[2]"Thus through faith they come to know God by an experimental knowledge. They have proved for themselves the reality of His word, the truth of His promises. They have tasted, and they know that the Lord is good.

"The beloved John had a knowledge gained through his own experience. He could testify: ... [cites 1 John 1: 1-31.

"So everyone may be able, through his own experience, to 'set his seal to this, that God is true' (John 3:33, ARV). He can bear witness to that which he himself has seen and heard and felt of the power of Christ. He can testify: 'I needed help, and I found it in Jesus. Every want was supplied, the hunger of my soul was satisfied; the Bible is to me the revelation of Christ. I believe in Jesus because He is to me a divine Saviour. I believe the Bible because I have found it to be the voice of God to my soul'" *(The Ministry of Healing,* p. 461*).*

Those of faith believe, through the study of the Bible, that God is the Person who created mankind in His own image, as personal counterparts who could enjoy mutual fellowship: "For whoever would draw near to God must believe that he exists and that he rewards those who seek him" (verse 6). The Biblical record awakens the intellectual awareness, but personal experience validates it. God truly "rewards" in ways that evoke even greater trust and commitment. The whole experience from awareness to commitment is all of faith—the *act* of the whole person.

They also know through experience that men and women can attempt to ignore God and reject His outstretched arms of reconciliation. Men and women of faith have also discovered that God does not turn away easily, that no one can long ignore Him. Because He is always making His presence known, they have learned that humanity can be responsible or irresponsible, but not unresponsible. "For what can be known about God is plain to them, because God has shown it to them…. So they are without excuse" (Romans 1:19). Everywhere, whatever the culture, mankind's haunting paradox of moral failure and suffocating pride point out the reality of humanity's lostness apart from God, apart from a faith-relationship with their Lord.

Human arrogance and mankind's searing awareness of guilt form the opposite of the faith experience. Adam and Eve's sin—the seed of all sin—was that they distrusted God. It was the beginning of human arrogance and rebellion. Genuine faith evaporated when they placed more trust in the Deceiver than in God. Their intellect, will and commitment turned to another who appealed to their perverted reason, self-indulgence, and self-assurance. Captivated intellectually, believing sincerely that the Deceiver might have something worth listening to, choosing to find out for themselves by tuning God out, permitting the Deceiver to persuade them that it all would work out for good—they unfolded a monstrous perversion of faith—faith misplaced, faith with a new person to trust. But from God's side such misplaced faith became distrust. And distrust plants strange seeds in human soil, seeds that cannot be merely "spoken away," even if forgiven. They were allowed to grow so that all concerned could see the consequences of "breaking faith" with God.

Distrust is rebellion—the opposite of faith. It fosters self-will, the antithesis of love. Rebellion, self-will, is sin. Sin destroys fellowship, smothers the conscience, and chokes hope. The only road back to all that has been lost through sin is the way of faith.

The gospel maps the route back. Paul stated that the aim of God's revelation, the purpose of Christian proclamation, was to awaken faith: "Now to him who is able to strengthen you according to my gospel and the preaching of Jesus Christ, according to the revelation of the mystery which was kept secret for long ages but is now disclosed and through the prophetic writings is made known to all nations, according to the command of the eternal God, to bring about the obedience of faith" (Romans 16:25, 26; see also 1:5).

Those who listen to the gospel discover that the road back to a peaceful, happy relationship with God *retraces* the steps of rebellion. Distrust becomes trust, rebellion becomes obedience, hate becomes love, independence becomes fellowship. But it is all of faith—this attitude that trusts, obeys, loves, and fellowships.

Faith, our response to God's initiative, is our personal act that corresponds to grace—God's personal act. God reveals Himself as a concerned, loving Lord. Yet His revelation truly fulfills its purpose only when those of faith call Him Lord and act accordingly. The grace of God remains thwarted until the faith of men and women accept the provisions of grace. They frustrate His grace until they act in the only way faith can—in trust and obedience toward God and in love toward others.

But as we stated earlier, Biblical faith does not make leaps of conviction merely on the basis of intuition, human reason, or deep emotion. Biblical faith—Noah's, Abraham's, Daniel's, Paul's—rested on persuasive objective evidence that what one believed was real. But we do not discover such "knowledge" of faith in the same way that we learn normal information. It is a special kind, *sui generis.* Faith's knowledge is not something that men and women acquire *on their own* but is, rather, a state, or experience, of being apprehended and challenged.

From one point of view, men and women of faith, instead of being the knowers, become the known, and God is the Knower. In other words, the knowledge of faith does not result from human logic, diligent scientific research, historical study, or even a probing of inner feelings and intuition. We may confirm the reality of faith by using any one or all the normal methods of discovering truth, but the knowledge of faith comes to men and women just as the knowledge of another person comes—through a personal confrontation, face-to-face, and not merely through newspaper clippings, the encouragement of mutual friends, or even letters exchanged.

In the God-man encounter, the meeting of grace and faith, men and women face their Creator, who also wants to be their Lord. When He says, "I am the Lord your God," He means, "You are My property." Suddenly there looms up the absurdity of created beings flaunting the counsel of their Creator and Lord.

But to understand God as Lord without knowing Him as Love would overpower men and women and drive them to profound despair. That is why Grace always comes through as the loving Lord, as the Father-God. We hear God call us sons and daughters and see a smile on His face, not condemnation (John 3:17).

But the knowledge of faith is more than the Good News learned about God. Faith also encounters the truth about mankind. In the act of faith, when we call God, Lord, at the same time we recognize ourselves as rebels who have insisted on our own way. "Thou art the Lord," faith says. "I belong not to myself but to Thee." In fact, no one truly believes he is lost, a rebel in need of help, without simultaneously saying "yes" to God and falling at His feet for pardon and power.

In other words, faith does not arise in the human experience until a person realizes his desperate need, his lost condition as he looks to the future, his powerlessness as he views the present, his guilt as he looks at the past. But a person does not comprehend his condition except through the personal experience of faith. Only then does a person accept God's analysis of the human predicament.

Everyone listens to the same message of human guilt and divine love from the "Loving Invader," whether it comes through the voice of conscience, the works of nature, historical providences, or the call of Scripture. Men and women of faith, however, permit God to break through their perimeter of arrogance and independence. The rebel rejects guilt and moral failure, explains it away, and remains his own lord. Those of faith accept the reality of their situation, that they are sinners who have turned their backs on their Creator and Lord, that hope in the Lord's mercy and power is exactly what they need.

Faith is the opposite of sin. Men and women of faith trust God and willingly obey Him. The sinner distrusts God and continues in his state of broken relationship, rebellion, and self-assertion. (See Romans 14:23.)

Peter's experience at Caesarea Philippi (Matthew 16) gives us an example of how faith develops, how intellectual conviction and heart commitment merge into a meaningful understanding of life. Biblical faith is not mere hope, not a blind resignation, not trust contrary to evidence. The experience of Christian faith is a rock on which men can make their decisions and build their futures without fear or anxiety. Peter and his colleagues were slowly learning all this, but at Caesarea Philippi the experience of faith took on a new focus. Many refer to that day as the beginning point of the Christian church. After all, why was Jesus able to change His teaching methods with His disciples after that momentous episode (Matthew 16:21)? Why was He able to make such astonishing promises on the basis of Peter's statement (verse 16), which at first looks rather tame and ordinary?

Our Lord's questions to Peter came at a decisive hour in His ministry. He and the twelve had just left Galilee after many pressing days of teaching, healing, and parrying with hostile church leaders who harassed them at every turn. But Jesus was now alone with His closest friends on earth, and He knew that time was running out.

If anyone would carry on His mission, such would have to come from His small group of twelve. Soon they would be the only visible link between God's plan of salvation and a lost world. They must herald His role as mankind's Saviour, Example, and Substitute to humanity. Did they themselves understand His mission? Were they convinced? Would their conviction be persuasive and convincing to others who had not even seen Jesus? After all, men and women were having difficulty understanding God when He Himself did the explaining. In such circumstances He put to His disciples for the first time, it seems, the question, "'But who do you say that I am?'" (Matthew 16:15).

Why does Jesus ask such a question? If He were not who He is, we would say that it was somewhat out of taste and smacked of conceit. Couldn't Jesus have simply stated who He was, if knowing who He was is the most important information in the world (John 17:3)? The fact that Jesus does not Himself declare His status leads us straight into the heart of the gospel and the meaning of faith.

Jesus presented a question rather than authoritatively declaring His Lordship because He knew that faith is never the result of mere instruction, no matter how much one knows of Biblical doctrine. That is, Biblical faith does not come at the end of a theological lecture or of a doctrinal argument. It is not something worked out in the head alone. That is why, after Peter's answer, Jesus could reply, "'Blessed are you, Simon Bar-Jona! For flesh and blood [that is, the normal earthly sources of human information] has not revealed this to you, but my Father who is in heaven'" (Matthew 16:17). If faith were the result only of knowledge, then those who do not pursue a theological degree at college and a graduate degree at a seminary would not have much chance.

When Peter said, "'You are the Christ, the Son of the living God'" (verse 15), he was responding to something more than physical evidence or logical arguments. For three years many thousands of people had heard much of what Peter had listened to. They had seen what Peter had seen. Yet those same thousands

21

helped to crucify Him whom Peter called Lord. In other words, most of those who *knew* more about Jesus than we ever will this side of His second coming never made the leap of faith.

Just to know about the historical Jesus—how He was born, what He did for thirty-three years, when He died, and even why—all may make a person doctrinally orthodox, but it is not yet faith. That is why Jesus asked the question, "But who do you say that I am?"

While other men and women saw only Jesus of Nazareth, Peter perceived Him as Lord. All that Jesus had said about Peter as a person had the ring of reality to it—every suggestion from Jesus that Peter followed in his own life had self-authenticating reality that spoke louder than the words themselves. Peter, representing his colleagues, called Jesus his Lord, not because he had special evidence denied to all others but because he was willing to give up his irrational freedom, his self-centered living, in obedience to One who spoke and acted as God.

Jesus could see that He had been breaking through to Peter's head and heart as He had not done with the multitudes. "Peter, you understand what I am trying to do. You now see that it would have been useless to proclaim Myself as God—many others have called themselves god. All I can do is reveal Myself as the Truth, and explain why I do what I do, and wait—wait for you to see and believe and trust! I must wait until faith is born!"

In Christ's reply to Peter's recognition we can see the inner process of true faith. Everyone, in some measure, has heard the voice of the "Father who is in heaven." But not all men and women respond to it as Peter did. Not all see themselves as guilty rebels in need of forgiveness and power, creatures lost without their Creator.

But for Peter it was decision time. He was ready to merge the Voice within with the external call that he discovered in Jesus of Nazareth. What Jesus was and said corresponded to the awareness in his heart. His affirmation of faith was that of a rebel capitulating. This fusing of inward conviction (based on the teaching, pleading voice of the Holy Spirit [Matthew 16:171) and outward evidence of the historical Jesus is the basis of Biblical faith.

We find Jesus today in the same way that Peter discovered God in Jesus. The question never gets old. The Timeless One towers over the wrecks of time, and the words come down through the years: "But who do you say that I am?"

"Only a teacher? Then you will write Me off as a mere ideal.

"Only a prophet? Then you will yet look for another to tell the truth about God, but you will not find him.

"But if I am God, then you cannot easily dismiss Me. If I am God, then what I say to you has more certainty than anything man can think up. However, it will mean nothing to you unless you are willing to trust Me. Only by listening to Me will you be sure about your own personal worth. And only by obeying Me will you be sure that what you are doing is meaningful, that life has a purpose. If you do not listen and obey, then you will never be sure about anything, ever."

Men and women of faith have learned all this. The foundation of faith is the Christian's personal relationship with Jesus of Nazareth, the Rock of faith.[3] But Jesus is no "rock" to those who do not call Him Lord. Yet for men and women of faith "the powers of death [hell] shall not prevail against" them (verse 18). That is why one could say about Jesus as He faced hell and death as no man has ever had to, "By faith, Christ was victor" *(The Desire of* Ages, p. 756). Only faith can set up a defense that Satan cannot penetrate.

The rock of faith must be a personal rock. Another's experience will not do. The faith that keeps its balance when the storms roll in and everything on earth seems to disintegrate has nothing

---

[3]"The truth which Peter had confessed is the foundation of the believer's faith.... There was only a handful of believers, against whom all the power of demons and evil men would be directed; yet the followers of Christ were not to fear. Built upon the Rock of their strength, they could not be overthrown.... Peter had expressed the truth which is the foundation of the church's faith, and Jesus now honored him as the representative of the whole body of believers.... The Rock of faith is the living presence of Christ in the church. Upon this the weakest may depend, and those who think themselves the strongest will prove to be the weakest, unless they make Christ their efficiency" *(The Desire of Ages,* pp. 412-414).

that someone else can borrow. The oil that the foolish brides-maids (Matthew 25) tried to obtain was the faith of their companions. They learned to their sorrow that one must build his own faith just as one must do his own breathing.

Such faith transforms men and women. It is more than an intellectual experience, more than an emotional high. Faith changes the whole person—whatever he thinks, however he relates to anybody he meets, whether man or God. Even today faith makes possible fresh witnesses to Paul's observation: "If any one is in Christ, he is a new creation" (2 Corinthians 5:17). In other words, faith is more than merely believing—it is a happening. Something far more than thinking and feeling occurs in faith. A new power, a new principle of action, takes over a person's life.[4]

That is why it could be said so plainly about Biblical faith: "A nominal faith in Christ, which accepts Him merely as the Saviour of the world, can never bring healing to the soul. The faith that is unto salvation is not a mere intellectual assent to the truth. He who waits for entire knowledge before he will exercise faith cannot receive blessing from God. It is not enough to believe *about* Christ; we must believe *in* Him. The only faith that will benefit us is that which embraces Him as a personal Saviour; which appropriates His merits to ourselves. Many hold faith as an opinion. Saving faith is a transaction by which those who receive Christ join themselves in covenant relation with God. Genuine faith is life. A living faith means an increase of vigor, a confiding trust, by which the soul becomes a conquering power" *(The Desire of Ages*, p. 347).

Biblical faith, then, is man's proper response to God's initiative. Those of faith are converted rebels. Thinking and agreeing with God is not enough, nor is feeling warm about Him sufficient. Merely telling the world that Jesus was God and the Lord of the universe and that He has forgiven all transgressors will not make men and women savable.

---

[4]"There is in genuine faith a buoyancy, a steadfastness of principle, and a fixedness of purpose that neither time or toil can weaken" *(Christ's Object Lessons*, p. 147).

Our lives demonstrate Biblical faith in the world of being and doing, not just on the front porch of intellectual belief. "It is not enough for us to believe that Jesus is not an impostor, and that the religion of the Bible is no cunningly devised fable. We may believe that the name of Jesus is the only name under heaven whereby men may be saved, and yet we may not through faith make Him our personal Saviour. It is not enough to believe the theory of truth. It is not enough to make a profession of faith in Christ and have our names registered on the church roll. 'He that keepeth His commandments dwelleth in Him, and He in him. And hereby we know that he abideth in us, by the Spirit which He hath given us.' 'Hereby we do know that we know Him, if we keep His commandments.' This is the genuine evidence of conversion. Whatever our profession, it amounts to nothing unless Christ is revealed in works of righteousness.

"The truth is to be planted in the heart. It is to control the mind and regulate the affections. The whole character must be stamped with the divine utterances. Every jot and tittle of the word of God is to be brought into the daily practice" (*Christ's Object Lessons*, p. 314).[5]

To put it plainly, living in faith is living as Jesus did. Living in faith develops the character of Jesus. Reflecting the character of Jesus is the aim of faith.

---

[5]"In all who will submit themselves to the Holy Spirit a new principle of life is to be implanted; the lost image of God is to be restored in humanity... A profession of faith and the possession of truth in the soul are two different things. The mere knowledge of truth is not enough. We may possess this, but the tenor of our thoughts may not be changed. The heart must be converted and sanctified ... True obedience is the outworking of a principle within. It springs from the love of righteousness, the love of the law of God. The essence of an righteousness is loyalty to our Redeemer. This will lead us to do right because it is right—because right doing is pleasing to God" *(ibid., pp. 96-98)*.

Chapter Four

FAITH, THE ONLY CONDITION OF SALVATION

PERHAPS the clearest formula of salvation, the classic expression of how men and women are saved, is Paul's statement: "For by grace you have been saved through faith" (Ephesians 2:8). But because humanity has misunderstood the nature and function of faith, this formula has been the crux of innumerable controversies, involving even the torture and death of millions. Satan is furious when truth is simple and clear, pleased when we pervert it.

We see the confusion highlighted when the Roman Catholic, the Calvinist, the Lutheran, and the Wesleyan Methodist attempt to explain that text to each other.

The passage, however, states that salvation does not result from either grace or faith alone. Salvation is not all God's part, nor is it all man's. If it were by grace alone, then it cannot be by faith. On the other hand, if faith solely provided us salvation, we would not need grace—unless we make up new definitions for faith and grace that Bible writers were not aware of

The ellipse of salvation-truth with its foci of grace and faith must not be manhandled and thus reconfigured. To make the ellipse of salvation-truth into a circle, overemphasizing one focus or the other, destroys the ellipse of truth. To over-emphasize grace or faith is to distort both—and we have "another gospel" (Galatians 1: 6, KJV).

Paul simply says that faith is the condition that makes salvation possible. Faith is not the cause—*grace* is. Although faith does not possess merit in itself, the absence of faith frustrates grace. Though grace is the source of salvation, we can have no salvation without faith.

Grace is whatever God has done, is doing, and will do for mankind. Our human minds cannot fathom what it all means. Biblical writers have tried to express the height and depth of grace with many terms and analogies: e.g., judicial actions in courts of law, vine and branches, sanctuary sacrifices, war prizes. None of the terms or analogies tell the whole story—they illustrate just certain aspects of it. Grace is whatever men and women need in order to be saved. It is exactly what men and women do not have, nor ever will have, of themselves.

Thus grace meets men and women in their need. But in God's plan, it cannot by itself save men and women. Men and women must do something as well—they must *respond* to grace. Becoming aware of their need, an awareness that grace itself has awakened, they can appropriate for themselves the help that grace offers. Faith is that appropriation, or acceptance, of grace that permits it to do its work in the life of the sinner. Thus faith permits grace to work.[1]

Properly understood, Paul's definition of how God saves men and women should have served as a barrier against two monstrous perversions that have divided Christian churches: (1) antinomianism, the concept that the law of God no longer has any binding on men and women of faith (and several variations of this position exist such as: a) you don't have to keep the law; b) you can't keep the law, if you tried; c) you should not try to keep the law and be a legalist); (2) righteousness by works, the concept that even worthy acts in some way either earn God's love, satisfy

[1] "Genuine faith appropriates the righteousness of Christ, and the sinner is made an overcomer with Christ; for he is made a partaker of the divine nature, and thus divinity and humanity are combined."

"In order to meet the requirements of the law, our faith must grasp the righteousness of Christ, accepting it as our righteousness. Through union with Christ, through acceptance of His righteousness by faith, we may be qualified to work the works of God, to be colaborers with Christ. If you are willing to drift along with the current of evil, and do not cooperate with the heavenly agencies in restraining transgression in your family, and in the church, in order that everlasting righteousness may be brought in, you do not have faith. Faith works by love and purifies the soul. Through faith the Holy Spirit works in the heart to create holiness therein; but this cannot be done unless the human agent will work with Christ" *(Selected Messages,* Book

God's love, meet the demands of justice, or help to secure salvation.

Those who have unfortunately emphasized grace in Paul's formula at the expense of reducing the responsibility of faith have misunderstood God's sovereignty and man's responsibility. In such thinking, faith tends to become a passive acceptance of what God has done. For them, man's accountability lies in intellectually accepting His marvelous gift, rejoicing in the fact that Jesus has paid the price, and that nothing more is necessary for a person's salvation. Logically and ethically (history so sadly reveals) such thinking leads to a lessened regard for disciplined, obedient concern for growth in character and a diminished emphasis upon the role of the Holy Spirit in mankind's salvation.

Those who have mistakenly overemphasized faith in Paul's formula have over estimated the ability of men and women to do good unaided by grace. Failing to grasp the magnitude and depth of sin, they believe that a divine spark of goodness lodges in everyone, merely waiting for the grace of God to fan it. They assume that mankind needs the Teacher more than the Saviour.

Dietrich Bonhoeffer spoke out plainly against the two perennial theological errors that exist whenever Christians misunderstand grace and faith. "The truth is that so long as we hold both sides of the proposition together they contain nothing inconsistent with right belief, but as soon as one is divorced from the other, it is bound to prove a stumbling-block. 'Only those who believe [have faith] obey' is what we say to that part of a believer's soul which obeys, and 'only those who obey believe' is what we say to that part of the soul of the obedient which believes. If the first half of the proposition stands alone, the believer is exposed to the danger of cheap grace, which is another word for damnation. If the second half stands alone, the believer is exposed to the danger of salvation through works, which is also another word for damnation" *(The Cost of Discipleship, p. 58* [hardback], New York: The Macmillan Company, 1959).

In other words, faith is not a divine gift providing salvation to a preselected group but a possibility made available to everyone through grace (Titus 2: 11). Here John Calvin, and even more so his followers, have made their fateful mistake. Divine decree does not predetermine salvation. Nor is faith a special gift of grace prompting selected sinners to "accept" Christ.

Grace is not the irresistible power of God that "secures" or "assures" salvation for those selected to receive faith. God did not send it to make the lips of men and women praise Him while their minds and hearts continue to live in sin. The Lord did not extend grace to make sin acceptable to God but to make men and women acceptable to God by destroying sin. (See Acts 10:35). Helping God to accomplish the work of grace is the divine-human cooperation called faith.

The story of Esau and Jacob highlights how grace and faith meet. "There was no arbitrary choice on the part of God by which Esau was shut out from the blessings of salvation. The gifts of His grace through Christ are free to all. There is no election but one's own by which any may perish. God has set forth in His word the conditions upon which every soul will be elected to eternal life—obedience to His commandments, through faith in Christ. God has elected a character in harmony with His law, and anyone who shall reach the standard of His requirement will have an entrance into the kingdom of glory....

"Every soul is elected who will work out his own salvation with fear and trembling. He is elected who will put on the armor and fight the good fight of faith. He is elected who will watch unto prayer, who will search the Scriptures, and flee from temptation. He is elected who will have faith continually, and who will be obedient to every word that proceedeth out of the mouth of God. The *provisions* of redemption are free to all; the *results* of redemption will be enjoyed by those who have complied with the conditions" *(Patriarchs and Prophets,* pp. 207, 208*)*.

In other words, God initiates, men and women respond. God explains what has to be done, men and women cooperate. The Lord has the pardon and power, and He awaits the human will to grasp His hand. On His side it is all of grace, while on our side it is all of faith—faith that permits God's full authority to have His will done. The essence of the sanctuary doctrine, taught in Tabernacle symbolism and explained in New Testament proclamation is this grand ellipse of truth—"the lesson of pardon of sin, and power through the Saviour for obedience unto life" *(Education,* p. 36*).*

From the first whisper of grace inviting the sinner to seek the Saviour, through the period of growth, until the transformed sinner "reflects the image of Jesus fully" *(Early Writings,* p. 71), it is the same grace operating, pursuing its original objective of reconciling men and women unto Himself. Its object is changed humanity, "a new creation," "so that in him we might become the righteousness of God" (2 Corinthians 5:17, 21).[2]

Paul urged, "We entreat you not to accept the grace of God in vain." "Since we have these promises, beloved, let us cleanse ourselves from every defilement of body and spirit, and make holiness perfect in the fear of God" (2 Corinthians 6: 1; 7: 1).

From the first response of faith, declaring our wretchedness and need, accepting God's pardon (the experience of justification), through our growth in grace (the experience of sanctification), until the Christian maturity reveals "the measure of the stature of the fullness of Christ" (Ephesians 4:13)—it is the same faith operating.

Biblical writers do not teach any distinction in grace or in faith between their functions in justification and sanctification. The apparent difference is not in kind but in degree.

Scripture sees grace speaking to a sinner offering pardon and acceptance. It views grace offered to men and women of faith as

---

[2]"God was to be manifest in Christ, 'reconciling the world unto Himself' 2 Corinthians 5:19. Man had become so degraded by sin that it was impossible for him, in himself, to come into harmony with Him whose nature is purity and goodness. But Christ, after having redeemed man from the condemnation of the law, could impart divine power to unite with human effort. Thus by repentance toward God and faith in Christ, the fallen children of Adam might once more become 'sons of God.' 1 John 3:2" *(Patriarchs and Prophets,* p. 64).

"It is the work of conversion and sanctification to reconcile men to God, by bringing them into accord with the principles of His law ... Through the merits of Christ he can be restored to harmony with his Maker. His heart must be renewed by divine grace; he must have a new life from above" *(The Great Controversy,* p. 467).

power to overcome sin, to develop a positive, Christlike character. Grace (God's initiative to save men and women from their sins) is always pardon and power for as long as man needs them until Jesus comes. Paul said it clearly: "Let us then with confidence draw near to the throne of grace, that we may receive mercy and find grace to help in time of need" (Hebrews 4:16).

Faith accepting pardon (knowing that a person can do nothing to earn it) is, at first, a passive response—faith extends its empty, needy hands for the mercies of God. But by accepting and cooperating with grace in overcoming hereditary and cultivated tendencies to sin, one assumes an active response. We are not describing two kinds of faith any more than two sides of a sheet of paper become two separate pieces. The same faith accepts pardon and power because such gifts are exactly what faith knows it needs. Regardless of its function in either justification or sanctification, faith is still the act of the whole person, not merely a mental acceptance of, or agreement with, what God wants to do to save us from our sinful predicament.[3]

Although prompted and supported by God, faith is not His work but ours—the human response to God's call. For men and women to respond to Him in faith, God must wait. He cannot, by the nature of His own plan in creating men and women as free, moral agents, force faith. He can appeal to it, win it, but never coerce it.

Because God made us able-to-respond, we are *response-able,* that is, responsible. Faith is properly responding to God, the experience of the truly responsible man or woman.[4]

Consequently, faith is not a special quality all by itself It is not something in addition to trust, obedience, joy, or love. Rather,

---

[3]"Many concede that Jesus Christ is the Saviour of the world, but at the same time they hold themselves away from Him, and fail to repent of their sins, fail to accept of Jesus as their personal Saviour. Their faith is simply the assent of the mind and judgment to the truth; but the truth is not brought into the heart, that it might sanctify the soul and transform the character" *(Selected Messages,* Book One, pp. 389, 390).

[4]"Faith in Christ as the world's Redeemer calls for an acknowledgment of the enlightened intellect controlled by a heart that can discern and appreciate the heavenly treasure. This faith is inseparable from repentance and transformation of character. To have faith means to find and accept the gospel treasure, with all the obligations which it imposes!' (Christ's *Object Lessons,* p. 112).

faith is the term Biblical writers have given to describe the person who trusts, who obeys, who witnesses to his Lord with joy, who proves his experience to be genuine by the way he or she lives. Faith is the whole person doing everything that a grateful person can do to show gratitude, sincerity, and loyalty.

For that reason we speak of the experience of faith as God's way of reestablishing the reign of love. Faith is not genuine, is not complete, unless it produces a truly loving person.[5]

John Wesley said it often and well: "Faith itself, even Christian faith, the faith of God's elect, the faith of the operation of God, is still only the handmaid of love.... It is the grand means of restoring that holy love wherein man was originally created."[6]

Faith, then, is not only a passive acceptance of God's mercies but an active response to His provision of power to produce the works of love. "For through the Spirit, by faith, we wait for the hope of righteousness. For in Christ Jesus neither circumcision nor uncircumcision is of any avail, but faith working through love" (Galatians 5:5, 6). We cannot say it too often: Faith is not an end in itself—it is God's means whereby the rebel becomes a loving, obedient son or daughter.

Christian love offers evidence that a person "is born of God and knows God" (1 John 4:7). "Love is the fulfilling of the law" (Romans 13:10; see also Galatians 5:14). Could Paul make it any clearer? "By grace you have been saved through faith"—that works through love.

Thus, through the life of faith the universe sees the intrinsic reality of the plan of salvation manifested, validated, and vindicated. When God goes about saving men and women, it is an ethical matter and not merely judicial and impersonal.

---

[5]"Genuine faith always works by love. When you look to Calvary it is not to quiet your soul in the nonperformance of duty, not to compose yourself to sleep, but to create faith in Jesus, faith that will work, purifying the soul from the slime of selfishness. When we lay hold of Christ by faith, our work has just begun. Every man has corrupt and sinful habits that must be overcome by vigorous warfare. Every soul is required to fight the fight of faith. If one is a follower of Christ, he cannot be sharp in deal, he cannot be hardhearted, devoid of sympathy. He cannot be coarse in his speech. He cannot ... use harsh words, and censure and condemn. The labor of love springs from the work of faith" (EGW, *6 BC*, p. 1111).

[6]*Works*, Vol. V, pp. 462, 464.

Because of the ethical transformation in genuine faith, salvation by faith "strikes at the root"[7] of all distortions in Christianity. It exposes the errors in even the good intentions of the penitential system and its quantifying of sin and the moral life inherent in the Roman Catholic system. It also points out the extreme overreaction during the Reformation periods wherein "by faith alone" meant "by no human effort," with the resulting reduction of human responsibility.

The Catholic error and the excesses in the Protestant overkill both missed the meaning of *faith* because they rarely saw it in its moral, total-person dimension. The Reformers tended to emphasize God's grace and the objective atonement while overlooking God's plan to save men and women by changing rebels into obedient, Christ-reflecting sons and daughters. For too many, salvation became abstract, intellectual, and sterile, especially in using terms such as justification as an event shorn of human responsibility. If saving faith "happens!' either as the result of divine decree or even as the outcome of "accepting" and "professing" a theological idea (doctrine), then it strangely lacks the Biblical element of moral responsibility and uncoerced "holy living."[8]

The "works" of human responsibility inherent in Biblical faith are exactly contrary to the "works of the law" that Paul and the Scriptures in general so strongly condemn (Galatians 2:16; Romans 3:28). The self-righteous works of one who seeks to earn God's approval, the quantifying of sin and the rituals that attempt to balance off so much sin with so much of good works are all a million light-years away from the "faith working through love" (Galatians 5:6), the faith of him or her "doing the will of the Father" (Matthew 7:21), "keeping the commandments of God" (1 Corinthians 7:19), putting "on the new nature, which is being

---

[7]*Ibid.*, p. 15.

[8]"It is not enough for us to believe that Jesus is not an impostor, and that the religion of the Bible is no cunningly devised fable. We may believe that the name of Jesus is the only name under heaven whereby man may be saved, and yet we may not through faith make Him our personal Saviour. It is not enough to believe the theory of truth. It is not enough to make a profession of faith in Christ and have our names registered on the church roll.... Whatever our profession, it amounts to nothing unless Christ is revealed in works of righteousness!' (*Christ's Object Lessons*, pp. 312, 313).

renewed in knowledge after the image of its creator" (Colossians 3:10).

The works of faith validate the genuineness of faith. "So faith by itself, if it has no works, is dead." "Faith was completed by works." "A man is justified by works and not by faith alone [*faith* being understood merely as an intellectual belief]" (James 2:17, 22, 24).[9]

The Holy Spirit prompts such works of faith.[10] Paul first describes them negatively: "Put to death therefore what is earthly in you [a list follows of those attitudes, habits, practices, that must be eliminated in the Christian's life]" (Colossians 3:5–10).

Then Paul portrays in positive terms the lifestyle of the genuine Christian: "Put on then, as God's chosen ones, holy and beloved, compassion, kindness, lowliness, meekness, and patience, forbearing one another and, if one has a complaint against another, forgiving each other... Above all these, put on love, which binds everything together in perfect harmony... And whatever you do, in word or deed, do everything in the name of the Lord Jesus, giving thanks to God the Father through him" (verses 12-17).

In Colossians 3 Paul depicts the life of faith in terms of the works of faith. He does so without using the words *justification*, *sanctification*, or *faith*. But his meaning is clear—without a

---

[9]"In order for man to be justified by faith, faith must reach a point where it will control the affections and impulses of the heart; and it is by obedience that faith itself is made perfect" *(Selected Messages,* Book One, p. 366).

"It is not faith that claims the favor of Heaven without complying with the conditions on which mercy is to be granted" *(The Desire of Ages,* p. 126).

"It is through faith that spiritual life is begotten, and we are enabled to do the works of righteousness!" *(ibid.,* p. 98).

[10]"To those that ask Him, Jesus imparts the Holy Spirit; for it is necessary that every believer should be delivered from pollution, as well as from the curse and condemnation of the law. Through the work of the Holy Spirit, the sanctification of the truth, the believer becomes fitted for the courts of heaven; for Christ works within us, and His righteousness is upon us.... By beholding Jesus we receive a living, expanding principle in the heart, and the Holy Spirit carries on the work, and the believer advances from grace to grace, from strength to strength, from character to character. He conforms to the image of Christ, until in spiritual growth he attains unto the measure of the full stature in Christ Jesus. Thus Christ makes an end of the curse of sin, and sets the believing soul free from its action and effect" *(Selected Messages,* Book One, p. 395).

changed life, without a "new creation," without a life-style that reflects increasingly the character of Jesus, the professed Christian is not a genuine Christian. "Without faith it is impossible to please him" (Hebrew 11:6).

In other words, how a person gets "right" with God is an ethical matter, far above the judicial plane. Unfortunately the Christian church has often lapsed into cheap concepts of God's mercy and grace. Psychologically, men and women find it easier to believe that God will forgive (justify) them *unconditionally,* that Jesus has done all the obedience necessary for their salvation. But such is not the message of the New Testament.

Faith is not merely acknowledgment that God has saved a person but also a grateful submission of the total person. God appeals not only to his or her intellect and emotion but also to the will and heart.[11]

Although Jesus died for everyone, God does not pardon (that is, justify) everyone. He extends no blanket amnesty to all sinners.

In 1977 the American President granted pardon to many military draft evaders. It was unconditional, requiring no change of heart, and probably not producing any. The forgiven draft evader was probably the same after the pardon as he was before.

God does not extend an unconditional pardon. He pardons only the penitent, justifies only those who have come to Him in faith (Romans 3:26).[12]

The changed attitude toward God and His law, toward self-indulgence and the needs of others, provides evidence that a life of faith exists. Such an attitude toward God shows that He has already justified that person—because He "justifies him who has

---

[11]"When Jesus speaks of the new heart, He means the mind, the life, the whole being.... What is the sign of a new heart?—a changed life" (*God's Amazing Grace,* p. 100).

[12]"There are conditions to our receiving justification and sanctification, and the righteousness of Christ" (*Selected Messages,* Book One, p. 377).

"Christ pardons none but the penitent, but whom He pardons He first makes penitent" (*ibid.,* pp. 393, 394).

faith in Jesus!' (Romans 3:26). Pleased and eager to pardon such people, He freely justifies them.

When God pardons, it is not "legal fiction."[13] God does not declare a sinner "justified" if he or she remains spiritually dead in sin. He does not pronounce a person "right" before Him if the person is a rebel, partially or wholly—*that* would be a legal fiction.

Although the truly justified person is righteous before God because of Christ's covering merits, he is not a truly righteous person substantively, that is, without sinful habits that need cleansing. Justification (pardon) does not *make* a person's character righteous. When God declares a person right or "justified," He recognizes the penitent response of faith, the beginning of a new relationship. Justification (pardon) starts a life program that will increasingly change the actual condition or state of the Christian's character.

When God justifies, (1) He recognizes faith in the change of heart (Romans 3:26); (2) He sends peace to the penitent (Romans 5:1); (3) He implants in the heart of faith a new life principle (Hebrews 10:16, 17; Ezekiel 36:26, 27); and (4) He begins the work of cleansing that will eventually fit the man or woman of faith for heaven (1 John 1:9).[14]

God does not pardon as men do. On one hand He does not wait for men and women to develop a righteous character before He will pardon them. He knows that no man or woman on their own can become "right" before Him (that is, acquire a righteous character). No unaided human effort, no matter how sincere, can storm the courts of divine justice with a perfect life, with a record of merit.

Nor does God come halfway by trading off a portion of righteousness for a portion of good works done by sincere men

---

[13]W Sanday and A. C. Headlam, *Romans, International Critical Commentary* (New York: Scribners, 1902) p. 367.

[14]"Christ the Restorer plants a new principle of life in the soul, and that plant grows and produces fruit. The grace of Christ purifies while it pardons, and fits men for a holy heaven" (That I *May Know Him*, p. 336).

and women (Matthew 7:21-27). Gifts, no matter how great, habitual, or sacrificial, can never bribe Him.

On the other hand He does not pardon unconditionally. He expects a change before He pardons, or else the integrity of His government would disintegrate. That change He has called faith. But it is not faith plus something else—that is, faith plus ritual law-keeping, or faith combined with rigorous self-mortification. "These have indeed an appearance of wisdom in promoting rigor of devotion and self-abasement and severity to the body, but they are of no value in checking the indulgence of the flesh" (Colossians 2:23). No, He wants just faith—the wholehearted response of a penitent (repentant) rebel who has capitulated. A rebel who has heard his or her heavenly Father whisper, "Son," "Daughter." One who clings to his or her new status, who pleads with the Father for help, power, protection, so that he or she will not dishonor the family name ever again. Only Jesus can give us power to obey, power to flee from selfish habits, power to overcome, power to be Father-pleasers—power to live the life of faith. [15]

"To be pardoned [justified] in the way that Christ pardons, is not only to be forgiven, but to be renewed in the spirit of our mind. The Lord says, 'A new heart will I give unto thee.' The image of Christ is to be stamped upon the very mind, heart, and soul. The apostle says, 'And we have the mind of Christ.' Without the transforming process which can come alone through divine power, the original propensities to sin are left in the heart in all their strength, to forge new chains, to impose a slavery that can never be broken by human power. But men can never enter

---

[15]"There are conscientious souls that trust partly to God, and partly to themselves. They do not look to God, to be kept by His power, but depend upon watchfulness against temptation, and the performance of certain duties for acceptance with Him. There are no victories in this kind of faith. Such persons toil to no purpose; their souls are in continual bondage, and they find no rest until their burdens are laid at the feet of Jesus.

"There is need of constant watchfulness, and of earnest, loving devotion; but these will come naturally when the soul is kept by the power of God through faith. We can do nothing, absolutely nothing, to commend ourselves to divine favor. We must not trust at all to ourselves nor to our good works; but when as erring, sinful beings we come to Christ, we may find rest in His love. God will accept every one that comes to Him trusting wholly in the merits of a crucified Saviour.

heaven with their old tastes, inclinations, idols, ideas, and theories" (EGW, *RH,* August 19,1890).

The Lord of heaven, who has been grieved for millennia as He has watched the seeds of sin bear bitter fruit, does not play word games with His children. The issue has always been faith or rebellion, obedience or disobedience, love or self-centeredness. That is why merely declaring it so will not remove sin. He does not justify (that is pardon) them as the kings and presidents of earth do draft evaders or common criminals.

The Lord of heaven wants an end to sin as soon as possible, and He has promised the resources of Heaven to assist those who feel the same way about their sins. Those who hate sin and want its reign to end are men and women of faith. Such people God freely justifies when they come to Him for pardon and power. [16]

Most Protestants and Catholics have had difficulty grasping the larger picture of the plan of salvation. "But forgiveness has a broader meaning than many suppose. When God gives the promise that He 'will abundantly pardon,' He adds, as if the meaning of that promise exceeded all that we could comprehend: 'My thoughts are not your thoughts, neither are your ways My ways, saith the Lord. For as the heavens are higher than the earth, so are My ways higher than your ways, and My thoughts than your thoughts.' Isaiah 55:7–9. God's forgiveness is not merely a judicial act by which He sets us free from condemnation. It is not only forgiveness *for* sin, but reclaiming *from* sin. It is the outflow of redeeming love that transforms the heart. David had the true conception of forgiveness when he prayed, 'Create in me a clean heart, 0 God; and renew a right spirit within me.' Psalm 51:10" *(Thoughts From the Mount of Blessing, p. 114).*

Love springs up in the heart. There may be no ecstasy of feeling, but there is an abiding, peaceful trust" *(Selected Messages,* Book One, pp. 353, 354).

[16]"Faith claims God's promises, and brings forth fruit in obedience. Presumption also claims the promises, but uses them as Satan did, to excuse transgression. Faith would have led our first parents to trust the love of God, and to obey His commands. Presumption led them to transgress His law, believing that His great love would save them from the consequences of their sin. It is not faith that claims the favor of Heaven without complying with the conditions on which mercy is to be granted. Genuine faith has its foundation in the promises and provisions of the Scriptures!' *(The Desire of Ages, p. 126).*

Justification (pardon) is "good news," but it does not exhaust the message of the gospel. It is the merciful undergirding of divine love throughout the Christian's growth. But for justification to be genuine, it must lead to a cleansing, a transformed experience. Such lives have a new face toward God (trust, obedience, loyalty), a new face toward mankind (love), and a new face toward themselves (self-appreciation and self-development for service rather than self-indulgence). [17]

In taking the first step toward *full* deliverance from sin, men and women of faith recognize that they are serious about their rebellion and want His grace to "save [them] ... from their sins" (Matthew 1:21). In justifying the sinner, God is recognizing the sinner's new faith.

Faith is our acceptance of God's willingness to justify, that is, His desire to "'forgive our sins and cleanse us from all unrighteousness" (1 John 1:9). Forgiveness and cleansing, pardon and power, are God's response to our trust, obedience, and loyalty (1 John 1:9; Hebrews 4:16; 1 Corinthians 1:18–24).

Truly "by grace ... [we] have been saved through faith.... For we are his workmanship, created in Christ for good works!' (Ephesians 2:8–10).

---

[17]"But while God can be just, and yet justify the sinner through the merits of Christ, no man can cover his soul with the garments of Christ's righteousness while practicing known sins, or neglecting known duties. God requires the entire surrender of the heart, before justification can take place; and in order for man to retain justification, there must be continual obedience, through active, living faith that works by love and purifies the soul.... In order for man to be justified by faith, faith must reach a point where it will control the affections and impulses of the heart; and it is by obedience that faith itself is made perfect" *(Selected Messages,* Book One, p. 366).

Chapter Five

FAITH CONDEMNS SIN IN THE FLESH

A S we noted in our opening pages, one day there will appear a group of people who will manifest the purpose of grace: they will "keep the commandments of God and [have] the faith of Jesus" (Revelation 14:12). They will, Jesus said, be overcomers "as I myself conquered" (Revelation 3:21). Such people have permitted grace to do its work because they learned through experience the meaning of faith: "This is the victory that overcomes the world, our faith" (1 John 5:4). Joyfully they sing, "Thanks be to God, who gives us the victory through our Lord Jesus Christ" (1 Corinthians 15:57).

Having been "born again" (John 3), that is justified (pardoned) by faith and continuing to be justified by faith, they now enjoy being sanctified by faith. The condition by which God pardoned them is the same by which they mature into a Christlike character—the condition of faith (Colossians 3:3). As soon as they were justified, the seed of a holy life (sanctification) began to grow.

Even if it were possible, it is not necessary to determine the time sequence between pardon and regeneration. We should avoid trying to categorize sharply the differences between, and the timing of, such phrases of Christian development as "justification," "regeneration," and "sanctification."[1] The same grace that awakens the sense of need and makes the sinner penitent brings peace and validates God's forgiveness through the Holy Spirit (Romans 5:1,5). It helps the sinner to see his need, and the

---

[1]Many commit the error of trying to define minutely the fine points of distinction between justification and sanctification. Into the definitions of these two terms they often bring their own ideas and speculations. Why try to be more minute than is Inspiration on the vital question of righteousness by faith?" (EGW, *6 BC*, p. 1072).

marvelous love of God draws him to ask in faith for God's power to put away sin and to live a holy life.

Becoming like Jesus is the goal of faith. Faith is the condition by which sinners become Christlike. Converted rebels manifest the working of "the power of God for salvation to every one who has faith" (Romans 1:16).[2]

Just as faith is the opposite of rebellion, so becoming like Jesus is the antithesis of sinful living. Jesus "condemned sin in the flesh" (Romans 8:3) chiefly because He did not sin "in the flesh." No one could accuse Him of sin (see John 8:46).

Christ proved that sin was not inevitable or necessary. He demonstrated by a life of faith that men and women when connected with divine power can live without sinning. He lived the life of faith so that the human family ever after would have reason for hope and cheer, so "that the righteousness of the law might be fulfilled in us, who walk not after the flesh, but after the Spirit" (Romans 8:4, KJV).

Paul is not romanticizing. The Holy Spirit was telling Him one of the basic truths of the gospel. As Jesus "condemned sin in the flesh," so likewise should His followers. Such is the challenge given to those who desire above all else to belong to that number "who keep the commandments of God and the faith of Jesus" (Revelation 14:12).

Jesus came to our world not only to live an exemplary life and die a substitutionary death but also to convince men and women that sin could be overcome, that God was not asking too much from the human family when He asked for total obedience, and that the power that kept Jesus from sinning would also sustain them. "God loved the world so dearly that He gave His only-begotten Son that whosoever would accept Him might have power to live His righteous life. Christ proved that it is possible for man to lay hold by faith on the power of God" *(Selected Messages,* Book One, p. 223).

[2]"The followers of Christ are to become like Him-by the grace of God to form characters in harmony with the principles of His holy law. This is Bible sanctification. This work can be accomplished only through faith in Christ, by the power of the indwelling Spirit of God" *(The Great Controversy,* p. 469).

The Lord wanted men and women to trust Him and to discover these facts for themselves, in their own experience. He desired for His people that they too could find the freedom of spirit that comes when the Spirit of God cooperates with faith, providing the power to overcome sin however manifested.[3] Only sinners are chained to the consequences of their poor choices.

To know all this demands more than intellectual exercise. It is a heart experience, the lifestyle of faith. The life of faith removes the power and pollution of sin, the condemnation of the law. Faith is the shield against all temptation, whether from without or from within. Take "the shield of faith, with which you can quench all the flaming darts of the evil one" (Ephesians 6:16).

Paul means "all." Condemning sin in the flesh is not a haphazard work. Either sin is destroyed completely, or it will triumph absolutely. Jesus did not partially condemn "sin in the flesh." His power today, given through the Holy Spirit, "is able to keep you from falling and to present you without blemish before the presence of his glory with rejoicing" (Jude 24).[4] That's His abiding promise!

There is something tragic about the professed Christian who nods in assent to all the teachings of his church, who believes that God loves him and promises to forgive him for his sons—and yet who knows little of God's power in his life. Such is the sad misunderstanding that many have of faith.[5] Unchanged traits of

---

[3]"He did not consent to sin. Not even by a thought did He yield to temptation. So it may be with us. Christ's humanity was united with divinity; He was fitted for the conflict by the indwelling of the Holy Spirit. And He came to make us partakers of the divine nature. So long as we are united to Him by faith, sin has no more dominion over us. God reaches for the hand of faith in us to direct it to lay fast hold upon the divinity of Christ, that we may attain to perfection of character" (The Desire of Ages, p 123).

[4]"The Spirit was to be given as a regenerating agent, and without this the sacrifice of Christ would have been of no avail. The power of evil had been strengthening for centuries, and the submission of men to this satanic captivity was amazing. Sin could be resisted and overcome only through the mighty agency of the Third Person of the Godhead, who would come with no modified energy, but in the fullness of divine power. It is the Spirit that makes effectual what has been wrought out by the world's Redeemer. It is by the Spirit that the heart is made pure. Through the Spirit the believer becomes a partaker of the divine nature. Christ has given His Spirit as a divine power to overcome all hereditary and cultivated tendencies to evil, and to impress His own character upon His church" (ibid., p. 671).

[5]"There are many who profess Christ, but who never become mature Christians. They admit

character dilute their declaration of faith, thus denying the saving virtue of Christ's power. The gospel is not for them "the power of God unto salvation" (Romans 1:16, KJV). They say that they have the truth about God, especially the truth about His last-day message to the world and what is soon to befall the earth, that they are "rich" with the truth. But such church members, until enlightened, "are wretched, pitiable, poor, blind, and naked" (Revelation 3:17). Sadly, they have not learned through the experience of faith what it means to follow Jesus all the way.

We ask again, What kind of faith is it that condemns sin in the flesh? As one writer put it, "What kind of faith is it that overcomes the world? It is that faith which makes Christ your own personal Saviour—that faith which, recognizing your helplessness, your utter inability to save yourself, takes hold of the Helper who is mighty to save, as your only hope. It is faith that will not be discouraged, that hears the voice of Christ saying, 'Be of good cheer, I have overcome the world, and my divine strength is yours'" *(The Review and Herald,* August 26, 1890).

The appeal to the Laodicean in Revelation 3 is not only to observe his or her great need but to open the door to all the provisions of the gospel, to eat with Jesus. We don't stop sinning because we fear God's punishment. We ask for His powerful grace because we don't want to disappoint Him.

Drawing nourishment from His presence, His power, His promises, the Laodicean can cheerfully rest assured that he may conquer and sit with Jesus in heavenly places. But the sitting will come only after the conquering only after the Laodicean conquers as Jesus conquered (Revelation 3:20, 21).[6]

---

that man is fallen, that his faculties are weakened, that he is unfitted for moral achievement, but they say that Christ has borne all the burden, all the suffering, all the self-denial, and they are willing to let him bear it. They say that there is nothing for them to do but to believe; but Christ said, 'If any man will come after me, let him deny himself, and take up his cross, and follow me.' Jesus kept the commandments of God" *(RH, June 17, 1890).*

"The pleasing fable that all there is to do is to believe, has destroyed thousands and tens of thousands, because many have called that faith which is not faith, but simply a dogma. Man is an intelligent, accountable being; he is not to be carried as a passive burden by the Lord, but is to work in harmony with Christ. Man is to take up his appointed work in striving for glory, honor, and immortality... Man can never be saved in disobedience and indolence" *(RH, April 1, 1890).*

The door of faith is open to all. Faith is the condition of salvation, the experience of those who "condemn sin in the flesh" and overcome as Jesus Himself conquered (verse 21). Faith believes, trusts, and lives on the promise that Jesus indeed shall "save his people from their sins" (Matthew 1:21).

[6]"These are the words of our Substitute and Surety. He who is the divine Head of the church, the mightiest of conquerors, would point his followers to his life, his toils, his self-denials, his struggles, and sufferings, through contempt, through rejection, ridicule, scorn, insult, mockery, falsehood, up the path of Calvary to the scene of the crucifixion, that they might be encouraged to press on toward the mark for the prize and reward of the overcomer. Victory is assured through faith and obedience.

"Let us make an application of the words of Christ to our own individual cases. Are we poor, and blind, and wretched, and miserable? Then let us seek the gold and white raiment that He offers. The work of overcoming is not restricted to the age of the martyrs. The conflict is for us, in these days of subtle temptation to worldliness, to self-security, to indulgence of pride, covetousness, false doctrines, and immorality of life" *(RH, July 24, 1888).*

Chapter Six

FAITH IS THE ANSWER— BUT WHOSE?

W E all have friends who have hit the wall. Perhaps we know all too well, personally what it is like to "hit the wall." No, not with your cars, nor in the middle of the night looking for the light switch.

But something like the long-distance runner, perhaps a marathoner, who at mile 21, loses sight of his goal. Fatigued, disillusioned, strange thoughts come into the head: "What am I doing this for? I've run longer than most people ever run. Twenty-one miles is far enough anyhow. Where's the taxi?"

I know people who have "hit the wall" not very far from the finish line. They describe their experience as a loss of their normal disciplined control, deep depression, despair, loneliness. The feeling of "checking out" and never wishing to run again is a common experience.

But "hitting the wall" is not an experience known only to marathoners. We all have, at times, hit the wall of complex circumstances, interconnected problems involving other people in business or church life—and we feel that fatigue and disillusionment. We know what is wrong, but we can't seem to do anything about it. So we rationalize: "The problems are too big; one person can't make any difference; it's not my responsibility anyhow; why can't others see the problem and lend some support; why do I feel so alone?"

But, fortunately, some go through the wall and finish the race. Some don't. What's the difference? Usually We go through the wall only after we have listened to others who have been there too. The experienced runners are able to describe what to expect so that more inexperienced runners will understand what's happening, that they are not alone in a strange personal disaster. I have heard of some marathoners who detect when others are hitting the wall and run beside them, encouraging them along to the finish line.

Whatever it is in our lives that began well, we should want to finish—we want to complete what started out to be a great reason for running. We can think about many commitments—our professional best, our marriage, some church project, our responsibility to our children, etc. There isn't much more satisfaction in life than finishing well, or completing a job. The question is: What to do when you hit the wall! The answer: Listen to experienced runners.

For millions of Christians it has been listening to a few words our Lord left with us. H.M.S. Richards, a long-time religious broadcaster, kept a remarkably helpful, unending poem going at the close of his broadcasts, "Have Faith in God . . ." We find those words in Mark 11:22. But it seems to me those words have been, at times, part of the problem for some sensitive, serious Christians.

How do we know when we have enough faith in God to make a difference? Does it take a full bucket of faith to move a mountain? Or how much can you move with half a bucket? Gladly we all want to have more faith, especially when we are hitting the wall. How often we hear, "I know how I should feel, I want to feel that faith, but somehow I don't seem to have enough." For them, that text is more of a taunt than a help.

But let's look at that text again: It does not say, your answer lies in how much faith you can get into your mind or heart. Rather it says, more clearly seen in the Greek, "Hold fast to the faithfulness of God." Ah, that's a completely different direction to look for faith, not into your faltering heart as it stands at the wall—but at the faithfulness of God who has never failed.

Failure to trust God's faithfulness was Eve's problem. She hit the wall, doubted God, and took the nearest taxi. At the bottom of every sin, whatever its nature, is this: we trust our own feelings and judgment to be more right, more satisfactory for the moment, than the plain, simple wisdom of the Lord.

Where do we find release from the burdens of life? Where do we find wisdom for the decisions that stare us in the face when we do not see a clear path to walk? Where do we find the words and composure for those moments of confrontation that loving parents, or employers, or colleagues must make to be account-able for their responsibilities?

We find this wisdom and courage and strength by listening to the Runner who ran His race well, to that Runner who comes back to run beside us as we break through the wall together. (See Hebrews 12:1–3). We don't trust our faithfulness, we trust His faithfulness.

Others may lie to you, even close friends at times. Jesus will not because He is faithful.

Others may back off their commitments you are both involved in, leaving you in a tough position. Jesus will not because He is always faithful.

Noah built an ark because He had learned that God is faithful to fulfill His promises. Abraham did not leave the security of Haran because his pro-forma looked fantastic—he went to Canaan because He had learned that God was faithful and would not leave him on his own.

Read Hebrews 11 again and note that none of these great exploits depended on any person's great exuberance of faith-feeling. They did what they did because they trusted God's faithfulness, not their own. They made a life habit of saying "yes" to God—whatever He said, wherever He would lead.

Satan from the beginning has said: Doubt God's faithfulness. You know his question to Eve, "Hath God said? Are you sure that He really meant that? Are you sure that you are not taking an extreme view? Don't you think that you are taking those words too literally?"

Even hearing those questions from another tend to tone down our enthusiasm, our whole-hearted commitment. We begin to wonder, we pause, we rationalize, we start drowning in our perplexities, we go off and do foolish things with our time or money just to get our minds off the calm, cool, clear words of divine instruction.

How often we estimate our difficulties in the light of our own resources and not in the light of His resources. We look at our faith, not His faithfulness! Thus, we attempt so little, and often fail in the little we attempt. But, we say, after all, we are doing as well as most everybody else.

All of us are weak men and women. To forget this, even with our super-achieving records and steel will-powers, to forget that we are weak men and women, is to walk away from the very strength and wisdom that God wants to deposit in our personal bank account—as if it were not available.

All of God's giants—men and women of faith—have been weak men and women. But they did great things for Him because they trusted in His faithfulness, not their own. He always produces what He promises. Men and women of faith know this from experience. They have learned how, by God's grace, to break through "the wall."

Chapter Seven

FAITH, THE KEY TO THE "LAST GENERATION"

NO one can receive any greater commendation than to be part of that group of which God says, "Here are they that keep the commandments of God, and the faith of Jesus" (Revelation 14:12, KJV). Such people compose the "last generation" of God's church on earth. Men and women so described are no longer rebels. Comfortable with God's way of life, they delight to do His will. Friends know them as generous and forbearing as well as firm and disciplined. Their names stand for unselfishness, integrity, reliability, and fairness.

In fact, in a significant, symbolic sense, they have the name of Jesus "and his Father's name written in their foreheads!" (Revelation 14:1), and "in their mouth no lie was found, for they are spotless" (verse 6). God is not ashamed to place His signature on them. He stands behind the quality of His own product.

Faith has brought them to the point where God can without embarrassment introduce them as His trophies of grace, appealing through them to all men and women to take a good look at what His way of life is all about. Such people are the goal of redemption, the purpose of grace: "He chose us in him before the foundation of the world, that we should be holy and blameless before him. He destined us in love to be his sons through Jesus Christ, according to the purpose of his will, to the praise of his glorious grace"—"destined and appointed to live for the praise of his glory" (Ephesians 1:4, 6, 12).[1]

They are the last generation for which God has waited, His living witnesses of what happens to people who appropriate by faith (that is, who make a personal possession of) the righteous-ness of Christ.[2]

Through their exhibit of genuine faith, their reflection of their Lord's faith, the gospel takes on new validation. Only when His people reveal the truth about His power and the worthiness of His way of life will the church effectively preach the "gospel of the kingdom ... throughout the whole world, as a testimony to all nations; and then the end will come" (Matthew 24:14).[3]

Someday the last generation of God's church will demonstrate that Biblical faith is more than a passive acceptance of God's forgiveness, more than a high-sounding, emotionally packed word. They will declare in a clear, undeniable life-style that faith is not only an important factor in the Christian character but the all-embracing element that separates nominal church members from genuine Christians (see Matthew 25).

Faith is such a deciding factor because (1) the correct under-standing of righteousness by faith depends on a correct grasp of faith, and (2) understanding and experiencing righteousness by faith (that is, the right way for man to relate to God) determine the eternal destiny of everyone.

---

[1]"From the beginning it has been God's plan that through His church shall be reflected to the world His fullness and His sufficiency. The members of the church, those whom He has called out of darkness into His marvelous light, are to show forth His glory. The church is the repository of the riches of the grace of Christ; and through the church will eventually be made manifest, even to 'the principalities and powers in heavenly places! (Ephesians 3: 10), the final and full display of the love of God" *(The Acts of the Apostles,* p. 9).

[2]"Genuine faith appropriates the righteousness of Christ, and the sinner is made an overcomer with Christ, for he is made a partaker of the divine nature, and thus divinity and humanity are combined" *(RH,* July 1, 1890).

[3]"The only way the truth can be presented to the world, in its pure and holy character, is for those who claim to believe it, to be exponents of its power" *(ibid.,* February 25, 1890).

"Character is power. The silent witness of a true, unselfish, godly life carries an almost irresistible influence. By revealing in our own life the character of Christ we cooperate with Him in the work of saving souls. It is *only* by revealing in our life His character that we can cooperate with Him. And the wider the sphere of our influence, the more good we may do. When those who profess to serve God follow Christ's example, practicing the principles of the law in their daily life; when every act bears witness that they love God supremely and their neighbor as themselves, *then* will the church have power to move the world" *(Christ's Object Lessons,* p. 340, italics supplied).

Those who have the "faith of Jesus" in the last generation respond to the messages symbolized by the three angels of Revelation 14. They are ready for probation to close because they have allowed God to cleanse their hearts from all sin. Their life pattern is that of a commandment-keeper.[4]

The Bible makes it clear that "in order to be prepared for the judgment, it is necessary that men should keep the law of God. That law will be the standard of character in the judgment. The apostle Paul declares: 'As many as have sinned in the law shall be judged by the law, . . . in the day when God shall judge the secrets of men by Jesus Christ.' And he says that 'the doers of the law shall be justified.' Romans 2:12-16. Faith is essential ... [for] the keeping of the law of God; for 'without faith it is impossible to please Him.' And 'whatsoever is not of faith is sin.' Hebrews 11:6; Romans 14:23" *(The Great Controversy, p. 436).*

To be like Jesus is to be a commandment keeper. To be a commandment-keeper is to possess the "faith of Jesus." Thus, the last generation reveals the aim of redemption, the purpose of justification and sanctification. At last a group of people will demonstrate the nature of the gospel seed implanted in their heart by grace through faith.[5] "The gospel of Christ is the law exemplified in character" *(Maranatha, p. 18).*

The end of the world, the completion of the Gospel Commission, the return of Jesus—all depend upon the ripening of the harvest. When Christ's character is fully on display in the last generation, vindicating God's law and His honor,[6] He can do

---

[4]"This experience everyone who is saved must have. In the day of judgment the course of the man who has retained the frailty and imperfection of humanity will not be vindicated. For him there will be no place in heaven; he could not enjoy the perfection of the saints in light. He who has not sufficient faith in Christ to believe that he can keep him from sinning, has not the faith that will give him an entrance into the kingdom of God" *(RH,* March 10, 1904).

"Obedience to the laws of God develops in man a beautiful character that is in harmony with all that is pure and holy and undefiled. In the life of such a man the message of the gospel of Christ is made clear" *(Sons and Daughters of God, p. 42).*

[5]"Christ is seeking to reproduce Himself in the hearts of men; and He does this through those who believe in Him. The object of the Christian life is fruit bearing-the reproduction of Christ's character in the believer, that it may be reproduced in others!' *(Christ's Object Lessons,* p. 67).*

[6]"The very image of God is to be reproduced in humanity. The honor of God, the honor of Christ, is involved in the perfection of the character of His people" *(The Desire of Ages.* p. 671).*

nothing more to get the world's attention. The harvest reveals the fruits of faith and the bitter unfolding of rebellion.

Thus God waits for men and women of faith. They are His channels through whom He gives the last invitations of mercy to a world facing judgment.

God will not wait forever. He will have His people through whom He can work without embarrassment.[7] But until that day "Christ is waiting with longing desire for the manifestation of Himself in His church. When the character of Christ shall be perfectly reproduced in His people, then He will come to claim them as His own" *(Christ's Object Lessons, p. 69).*

The gospel harvest is the result of faith. The fully developed fruit of Christlike characters is not something imputed to God's people only. Hardly![8] They *are* men and women who have overcome "by the blood of the Lamb and by the word of their testimony" (Revelation 12:11). They know through experience "the faith that works by love and purifies the soul from every stain of sin" *(RH, June 10, 1890).* "John says, 'Beloved, now are we the sons of God, and it doth not yet appear what we shall be: but we know that, when he shall appear, we shall be like him; for we shall see him as he is.' It is no cheap faith that we are to have. 'Every man that hath this hope in him purifieth himself, even as he is pure'" *(ibid.).*

Living in the last generation as overcomers, as commandment-keepers and men and women of genuine faith, is not something that one can achieve as an ascetic or through any other lifestyle wherein individuals seek to escape the ordinary responsibilities of life. Jesus possessed a life of faith *amid* the duties and perils that face anyone who fulfills his responsibilities as a member of a family, an economic provider, or a good neighbor.

---

[7]"Clad in the armor of Christ's righteousness, the church is to enter upon her final conflict. 'Fair as the moon, clear as the sun, and terrible as an army with banners,' (Song of Solomon 6:10), she is to go forth into all the world, conquering and to conquer" *(Prophets and Kings, p. 725).*

[8]"The followers of Christ are to become like Him-by the grace of God to form characters in harmony with the principles of His holy law. This is Bible sanctification. The work can be accomplished only through faith in Christ, by the power of the indwelling Spirit of God" *(The Great Controversy, p. 469).*

Perhaps that is one of the reasons why God reminds us of Enoch and Elijah, men "of like nature with ourselves" (James 5:17). These two men did not see death. The Lord translated them. Their experiences have become examples of what awaits the last generation—the last generation of genuine faith.

Their lives teach that heaven will translate no one unless he or she has become an overcomer. "Enoch and Elijah are the correct representatives of what the race might be through faith in Jesus Christ if they chose to be. Satan was greatly disturbed because these noble, holy men stood untainted amid the moral pollution surrounding them, perfected righteous characters, and were accounted worthy for translation to Heaven" *(ibid.,* March 3, 1874).

Elijah achieved his victories as an overcomer because he was a great man of faith. God honored Enoch, translated him into the heavens, because he was a man of faith (Hebrews 11:5).[9] "The godly character of this prophet represents the state of holiness which must be attained by those who shall be 'redeemed from the earth' (Revelation 14:3) at the time of Christ's second advent.... Like Enoch, God's people will seek for purity of heart and conformity to His will, until they shall reflect the likeness of Christ" (*Patriarchs and Prophets,* pp. 88, 89).

In the last generation the issues of the great controversy stand out sharply—as clear as they were when Jesus of Nazareth met Satan head-on. Although Jesus proved that God was fair, loving, and just, that man on earth in his fallen condition could live as God wills by His grace—He now has chosen to wait for His church to demonstrate that all these statements are more than

---

[9]"Enoch's case is before us. Hundreds of years he walked with God. He lived in a corrupt age, when moral pollution was teeming all around him; yet he trained his mind to devotion, to love purity. His conversation was upon heavenly things. He educated his mind to run in this channel, and he bore the impress of the divine. His countenance was lighted up with the light which shineth in the face of Jesus. Enoch had temptations as well as we. He was surrounded with society no more friendly to righteousness than is that which surrounds us. The atmosphere he breathed was tainted with sin and corruption, the same as ours; yet he lived a life of holiness. He was unsullied with the prevailing sins of the age in which he lived. So may we remain pure and uncorrupted. He was a representative of the saints who live amid the perils and corruptions of the last days. For his faithful obedience to God he was translated. So, also, the faithful, who are alive and remain, will be translated" (*Testimonies,* Vol. 2, p. 122).

theological assertions, that the life of faith He lived and the character He manifested are possible for all men and women to reach.

Only such lives of faith will finally prove Satan's accusations wrong and God just in all His ways. (See Revelation 19:2.)

Some generation of church members will become God's faithful "last" one. They will confirm the triumph that was our Lord's—that men and women need not succumb to temptation—that the grace of God will sustain a spontaneous, habitual life of love and fidelity. It, too, is part of the Good News that honest, weary, struggling humanity wants to know. Sincere voices ask, "Is the battle worth it? In fact, is there such a thing as victory?"

Although they read that the life of Jesus says yes, the living witness of faith in the last generation will offer the crowning evidence that the Bible means what it says when it expresses in so many ways that God "is above to keep ... [them] from falling" (Jude 24).

Freedom from anxiety, from the physical and emotional consequences of guilt, from enslaving, self-destroying habits; freedom to rejoice in the present and to hope for the future—such a lifestyle is what yearning hearts the world over need. They have heard about it from a thousand pulpits, but it will not be convincing without the life that backs up the words proclaimed. Herein resided the authority of Jesus and so will it be in the lives of those "who keep the commandments of God, and the faith of Jesus."

Those living demonstrators of "faith working through love" (Galatians 5:6) will silence the mouth of all who depreciate God's law, His mercy, His justice. Such lives of faith will be the glory that completes the Gospel Commission, the light of truth that gives credibility to the word of truth.[10]

---

[10]"At this time the church is to put on her beautiful garments—'Christ our righteousness.' There are clear, decided distinctions to be restored and exemplified to the world in holding aloft the commandments of God and the faith of Jesus. The beauty of holiness is to appear in its native luster in contrast with the deformity and darkness of the disloyal, those who have revolted from the law of God....

Here at last are the people for whom God has waited—people who not only truly say "Yes" to everything He says but also demonstrate the distinctive quality of what happens to people who do say "Yes" to God.[11] "Since all these things are thus to be dissolved, what sort of persons ought you to be in lives of holiness and godliness, waiting for and hastening the coming of the day of God.... Therefore, beloved, since you wait for these, be zealous to be found by him without spot or blemish, and at peace" (2 Peter 3:11-14).

Not a rebel exists among them—they are men and women of faith.

"The church is firmly and decidedly to hold her principles before the whole heavenly universe and the kingdoms of the world; steadfast fidelity in maintaining the honor and sacredness of the law of God will attract the notice and admiration of even the world, and many will, by the good works which they shall behold, be led to glorify our Father in heaven. The loyal and true bear the credentials of heaven, not of earthly potentates....

"The Lord has provided His church with capabilities and blessings, that they may present to the world an image of His own sufficiency, and that His church may be complete in Him, a continual representation of another, even the eternal world....

"The church, being endowed with the righteousness of Christ, is His depository, in which the wealth of His mercy, His love, His grace, is to appear in full and final display... In their untainted purity and spotless perfection, Christ looks upon His people as the reward of all His. suffering, His humiliation, and His love, and supplement of His glory" (Testimonies to Ministers, pp. 16-19).

"The world today is in crying need of a revelation of Christ Jesus in the person of His saints. God desires that His people shall stand before the world a holy people. Why? Because there is a world to be saved by the light of gospel truth; and as the message of truth that is to call men out of darkness into God's marvelous light is given by the church, the lives of its members, sanctified by the Spirit of truth, are to bear witness to the verity of the messages proclaimed" (ibid., p. 458).

[11]"It is God's purpose to manifest through His people the principles of His kingdom....

"A great work is to be accomplished in setting before men the saving truths of the gospel. This is the means ordained by God to stem the tie of moral corruption. This is His means of restoring His moral image in man.... To present these truths is the work of the third angel's message....

"The glory of this light, which is the very glory of the character of Christ, is to be manifested in the individual Christian, in the family, in the church, in the ministry of the word, and in every institution established by God's people. All these the Lord designs shall be symbols of what can be done for the world. They are types of the saving power of the truths of the gospel....

"By beholding the goodness, the mercy, the justice, and the love of God revealed in the church, the world is to have a representation of His character. And when the law of God is thus exemplified in the life, even the world will recognize the superiority of those who love and fear and serve God above every other people on the earth!' (Testimonies, Vol. 6, pp. 9-12).

We invite you to view the complete
selection of titles we publish at:

www.TEACHServices.com

Scan with your mobile
device to go directly
to our website.

Please write or email us your praises, reactions, or
thoughts about this or any other book we publish at:

TEACH Services, Inc.
P U B L I S H I N G
www.TEACHServices.com ● (800) 367-1844

P.O. Box 954
Ringgold, GA 30736

info@TEACHServices.com

TEACH Services, Inc., titles may be purchased in bulk for
educational, business, fund-raising, or sales promotional use.
For information, please e-mail:

BulkSales@TEACHServices.com

Finally, if you are interested in seeing
your own book in print, please contact us at

publishing@TEACHServices.com

We would be happy to review your manuscript for free.